CONTENTS

Understanding They Aren't Judging you; they are judging themselves. — 1

Chapter 1: The Mirror Effect: Reflecting on Our Own Judgments — 3

Chapter 2: The Power of Self-Awareness: Embracing Vulnerability and Authenticity — 6

Chapter 3: Breaking the Cycle: Shifting from Criticism to Compassion — 10

CHAPTER 4: The Art of Forgiveness: Letting Go of Resentment and Anger — 13

Chapter 5: Grace Over Judgment: Choosing Kindness and Understanding — 16

Chapter 6: The Language of Self-Love: Transforming Negative Self-Talk — 19

Chapter 7: Cultivating Empathy: Stepping into Others' Shoes — 22

Chapter 8: Cultivating Mindfulness and Self-Reflection — 25

Chapter 9: The Journey of Self-Discovery — 28

Chapter 10: Embracing Imperfection — 31

Chapter 11: The Courage to Be Vulnerable — 34

Chapter 12: The Courage In Being Vulnerable — 37

Chapter 13: Cultivating Self-Compassion — 40

Chapter 14: Embracing Imperfection — 43

Chapter 15: The Healing Power of Forgiveness	47
Chapter 16: The Power of Gratitude	50
Chapter 17: Embracing Self-Compassion	53
Chapter 18: The Power of Boundaries	56
Chapter 19: The Power of Mindful Listening	59
Chapter 20: Finding Strength in Vulnerability	62
Chapter 21: Embracing the Journey of Self-Discovery	65
CHAPTER 22: The Power of Self-Reflection	69
Chapter 23: Embracing Imperfections and Practicing Radical Acceptance	72
Chapter 24: Nurturing Self-Connection	76
Chapter 25: The Power of Resilience	79
Chapter 26: The Journey to Self-Love	82
Desired Impact for Readers:	86
ABOUT THE AUTHOR	87

UNDERSTANDING THEY AREN'T JUDGING YOU; THEY ARE JUDGING THEMSELVES.

Adrianne Muntz

Copyright © 2024 Adrianne Muntz

All Rights Reserved.

CHAPTER 1: THE MIRROR EFFECT: REFLECTING ON OUR OWN JUDGMENTS

As humans, we are constantly making judgments. From the moment we wake up to the moment we go to bed, our minds are filled with thoughts and opinions about ourselves and others. These judgments often stem from our own insecurities and fears, projecting onto others what we struggle to accept within ourselves.

In this chapter, we will explore the mirror effect of judgment and self-awareness. We will delve into the source of our judgments, the importance of self-reflection and introspection, as well as the cultivation of empathy and compassion towards others.

It is essential for us to recognize that our judgments are not a reflection of reality but rather a projection of our own internal struggles. When we judge someone else's appearance or actions, it is often because those aspects trigger something within us that we find uncomfortable or unaccepted. By understanding this mirror effect, we can begin to unravel the layers of our own insecurities.

Self-reflection plays a pivotal role in breaking free from judgment. Taking time each day to introspect allows us to gain insight into why certain judgments arise within us. It enables us to understand where these beliefs come from – whether they are societal influences or past experiences – so that we can consciously question them. Through self-reflection, we begin to peel back the layers of conditioning and allow ourselves room for growth.

However, self-awareness is not just about recognizing our own judgments; it is also about developing empathy towards others. When we understand ourselves better – our fears, desires, and struggles – it becomes easier for us to extend compassion towards those around us who may be going through similar experiences. Empathy bridges the gap between judgment and understanding by reminding us that everyone has their own battles that they are fighting.

Cultivating empathy requires an open heart and a willingness to step outside of ourselves. It means actively listening without judgment when someone shares their story, and trying to understand their perspective even if it differs from our own. Empathy is not about agreeing with everything someone says or does; it is about acknowledging and validating their feelings, recognizing that they are valid and deserving of compassion.

By embracing self-awareness and cultivating empathy, we can break the cycle of judgment that often keeps us trapped in a cycle of negativity. When we judge others, we not only harm them but also ourselves. Judgment creates distance and separation, preventing us from forming authentic connections with others.

Understanding that empathy towards others starts with understanding ourselves allows us to approach relationships with grace rather than judgment. We can choose kindness over criticism when faced with challenging situations, recognizing that everyone is on their own journey and dealing with their unique set of circumstances.

The mirror effect of judgment reminds us that our judgments are often projections of our own insecurities. By practicing self-reflection and introspection, we can gain a deeper understanding of ourselves and why certain judgments arise within us. Cultivating empathy towards others allows us to extend grace instead of judgment in our interactions. Understanding They Aren't Judging you; they are judging themselves reminds us that compassion and understanding are crucial for breaking free from the cycle of judgment and fostering deeper connections in our lives.

CHAPTER 2: THE POWER OF SELF-AWARENESS: EMBRACING VULNERABILITY AND AUTHENTICITY

In the pursuit of self-discovery and growth, self-awareness serves as a beacon that illuminates the path to personal transformation. It is through self-awareness that we can begin to unravel the layers of our being, embracing vulnerability and authenticity along the way. This chapter delves into the power of self-awareness, highlighting its capacity to foster self-love and forgiveness.

At times, we find ourselves caught in a web of societal expectations and pressures. We strive to present an image of perfection, fearing that our vulnerabilities will be seen as weaknesses. However, it is in our vulnerability that true strength lies. By embracing our flaws and imperfections, we open ourselves up to authentic connections with others.

To cultivate a sense of self-awareness, we must first be willing to explore our inner landscape with curiosity and compassion. This requires creating a safe space for introspection – a sanctuary where judgment has no place. Whether through journaling or meditation, engaging in practices that allow us to observe our thoughts and emotions without attaching labels or criticisms can facilitate this process.

As we delve deeper into this journey of self-discovery, it is crucial to recognize that acceptance is not synonymous with complacency. We can acknowledge our shortcomings while still striving for personal growth. Self-awareness empowers us to identify areas where change is necessary without berating ourselves for past mistakes.

However, embracing vulnerability goes beyond acknowledging our weaknesses; it also entails cultivating profound self-love. In a world that often emphasizes external validation, it is easy for us to lose sight of our inherent worthiness. Yet when we embrace vulnerability and authenticity within ourselves, we create space for genuine love and acceptance.

Forgiveness plays an integral role in this process of embracing vulnerability and authenticity. Oftentimes, harboring resentment towards ourselves becomes an obstacle on the path toward personal growth. By forgiving ourselves for past mistakes and perceived failures, we release the emotional burdens that hinder our progress. Forgiveness is not about condoning or forgetting, but rather about freeing ourselves from the chains of resentment and anger.

To foster self-forgiveness, we can engage in practices such as writing forgiveness letters to ourselves or seeking support from trusted friends or therapists. By acknowledging our humanity and embracing compassion, we allow room for growth and healing.

Authenticity arises when we align our external expressions with our inner truth. It requires unwavering courage to live in accordance with our values, unapologetically showing up as who we truly are. Authenticity invites us to shed the masks society has placed upon us and embrace our unique qualities and passions.

In a world that often rewards conformity, choosing authenticity can be challenging. However, it is through authenticity that we find the freedom to express ourselves fully and create meaningful connections with others who appreciate us for who we genuinely are.

As this chapter comes to a close, let us reflect on the power of self-awareness in embracing vulnerability and authenticity. By embarking on this journey within ourselves, we unlock the key to self-love and forgiveness – essential ingredients for personal growth.

In "Understanding They Aren't Judging you, they are judging themselves," recognizing the mirror effect of judgment becomes paramount. Through self-awareness, vulnerability, and authenticity explored in this chapter, readers gain insights into their own judgments while cultivating empathy towards others' journeys of self-discovery. The power of understanding oneself paves the way for breaking free from criticism towards compassion – both towards oneself and others.

With each step taken on this path of self-awareness, readers will realize that judgment is often a reflection of one's own insecurities rather than an accurate assessment of others' worthiness. The journey continues as we explore the art of forgiveness, transforming negative self-talk, and cultivating empathy in the chapters to come.

CHAPTER 3: BREAKING THE CYCLE: SHIFTING FROM CRITICISM TO COMPASSION

In this chapter, we delve into the harmful effects of constant self-criticism and explore the transformative power of cultivating self-compassion. It is all too easy to fall into a pattern of judging ourselves harshly, but by shifting our mindset towards compassion, we can break free from this cycle and experience personal growth.

We live in a society that often values perfection and places immense pressure on individuals to meet unrealistic standards. As a result, many of us find ourselves constantly criticizing our own actions, appearance, and capabilities. This constant self-criticism not only erodes our self-esteem but also hinders our ability to grow and thrive.

To break free from this cycle of criticism, we must first recognize that it originates from within ourselves. Our judgments are often projections of our own insecurities or fears onto others. By acknowledging this source, we can begin to dismantle the negative narratives we have created about ourselves.

Practicing self-compassion is a powerful tool for personal growth. It involves treating ourselves with kindness and understanding, just as we would treat a dear friend or loved one. Rather than berating ourselves for perceived flaws or mistakes, we learn to offer ourselves love and forgiveness.

One way to cultivate self-compassion is through mindfulness and self-reflection. Taking the time to observe our thoughts without judgment allows us to gain insight into the patterns of negativity that hold us back. Through this practice, we can begin replacing critical thoughts with compassionate ones.

It's important to remember that practicing self-compassion doesn't mean excusing harmful behaviors or neglecting personal growth. Rather, it means approaching ourselves with kindness even when we make mistakes or fall short of expectations. By embracing compassion instead of criticism in these moments, we create space for growth and learning.

Breaking the cycle of criticism also involves reframing how we view failure and setbacks. Instead of seeing them as indicators of our worth or abilities, we can view them as opportunities for growth and resilience. Embracing a growth mindset allows us to approach challenges with curiosity and openness, rather than fear and self-judgment.

In addition to cultivating self-compassion, it is equally important to extend compassion towards others. We often judge others based on limited information or biased perceptions. However, by practicing empathy and understanding, we can challenge these judgments and foster deeper connections with those around us.

When we shift from criticism to compassion, we create

an environment that encourages personal growth and understanding. This not only benefits ourselves but also extends to our interactions with others. By choosing compassion over judgment, we create space for kindness and empathy in our relationships.

It's essential to remember that breaking the cycle of criticism takes time and patience. It requires a commitment to self-reflection, mindfulness, and self-compassion. As we continue on this journey of self-discovery and growth, let us embrace the power of compassion as a catalyst for positive change within ourselves and in our relationships.

Understanding They Aren't Judging you; they are judging themselves: Breaking Free from the Cycle of Criticism through Self-Compassion serves as an invitation for readers to explore their own patterns of self-criticism while offering guidance on how to cultivate self-compassion as a means for personal transformation. By shifting our mindset from judgmental criticism towards compassionate understanding - both towards ourselves and others - we can break free from the limitations of negativity and instead embrace a path filled with love, acceptance, and personal growth

CHAPTER 4: THE ART OF FORGIVENESS: LETTING GO OF RESENTMENT AND ANGER

In this chapter, we delve into the transformative power of forgiveness. We explore how practicing forgiveness can lead to inner peace and liberation from emotional burdens. By letting go of resentment and anger, we open ourselves up to healing and growth.

Forgiveness is a complex and multifaceted process. It involves acknowledging the pain caused by others, understanding our own role in the situation, and making a conscious decision to release negative emotions attached to it. It is not about condoning or forgetting what happened but rather freeing ourselves from the chains that keep us bound to the past.

One key aspect of forgiveness is recognizing that holding onto resentment only harms ourselves. When we hold onto anger, it consumes our thoughts, drains our energy, and hinders our ability to move forward. By forgiving, we release ourselves from this toxic cycle and create space for healing.

To embark on a journey of forgiveness, it is important to start with self-forgiveness. Often, we carry guilt or shame for our own actions or perceived shortcomings. We must learn to extend compassion towards ourselves in order to truly forgive others. Self-forgiveness allows us to break free from self-imposed limitations and embrace personal growth.

Practicing forgiveness requires courage and vulnerability. It means facing painful emotions head-on without suppressing or denying them. By allowing ourselves to fully experience these emotions, we create an opportunity for healing and transformation.

One effective strategy for letting go of resentment is through empathy towards those who have hurt us. Understanding that everyone carries their own wounds enables us to see beyond their actions or words directed at us. Recognizing that their behavior often stems from their own pain allows us to cultivate compassion instead of anger.

Another powerful tool in the art of forgiveness is gratitude. By focusing on what we are grateful for instead of dwelling on grievances, we shift our perspective towards positivity and abundance. Gratitude helps us find the silver lining in difficult situations and reminds us of the good that exists alongside the pain.

It is important to note that forgiveness does not always mean reconciliation or maintaining close relationships with those who have hurt us. Sometimes, forgiveness means creating healthy boundaries and choosing not to engage with individuals who continue to cause harm. Forgiveness is ultimately about finding peace within ourselves, regardless of external circumstances.

In order to truly let go of resentment and anger, we must also practice forgiveness towards ourselves. We all make mistakes and carry regrets, but self-forgiveness allows us to learn from these experiences rather than dwell on them. By acknowledging our imperfections with kindness and compassion, we create space for personal growth and self-acceptance.

As we navigate the journey of forgiveness, it is important to remember that it is not a linear process. Healing takes time and patience. Some wounds may require more time to mend than others, but by committing ourselves to the practice of forgiveness, we open up endless possibilities for growth and transformation.

The art of forgiveness is a powerful tool for letting go of resentment and anger. By embracing self-forgiveness, cultivating empathy towards others, practicing gratitude, setting healthy boundaries when necessary, and offering kindness towards ourselves in times of mistakes or regrets - we can experience true liberation from past pain. Through forgiveness, we create space for healing, personal growth, and inner peace.

The book title "Understanding They Aren't Judging you; they are judging themselves" beautifully connects with this chapter on forgiveness. As we learn to let go of resentments caused by others' judgments or criticisms towards us through practicing forgiveness - we understand that their judgments were never really about us but rather reflections of their own insecurities or struggles. By understanding this truth deeply within ourselves - we can break free from being affected by external judgment while extending empathy towards others' journeys as well

CHAPTER 5: GRACE OVER JUDGMENT: CHOOSING KINDNESS AND UNDERSTANDING

In this chapter, we delve into the importance of grace over judgment in our interactions with others. It is easy to fall into the trap of passing judgment on those around us, but by choosing kindness and understanding instead, we can create a more compassionate and harmonious world.

Often, when someone behaves in a way that triggers us or rubs us the wrong way, our immediate reaction is to judge them. We make assumptions about their intentions or character without taking the time to truly understand their perspective. However, it is important to recognize that everyone has their own unique journey and experiences that shape their behavior.

To choose grace over judgment means to approach every interaction with an open heart and mind. Instead of jumping to conclusions or making snap judgments, we can take a moment to pause and consider why someone might be acting the way they are. Perhaps they are going through a difficult time or facing challenges that we are unaware of.

Choosing kindness means extending empathy towards others, even when it may not be easy. It means being patient and understanding, allowing room for growth and change. When we choose kindness over judgment, we create an environment where people feel safe to be themselves without fear of criticism or rejection.

Understanding is another key aspect of choosing grace over judgment. By seeking to understand others' perspectives and experiences, we can foster deeper connections and promote empathy in our relationships. This requires active listening and putting ourselves in someone else's shoes – seeing things from their point of view rather than solely focusing on our own biases.

One effective strategy for choosing grace over judgment is practicing mindfulness. Mindfulness allows us to observe our thoughts without immediately reacting to them. By cultivating presence in the present moment, we can catch ourselves before passing judgment and consciously choose a more compassionate response.

Another helpful tool is reframing our thoughts about others. Instead of assuming negative intent behind someone's actions or words, we can give them the benefit of the doubt and assume positive intent. This shift in mindset can open up space for understanding and connection, rather than creating a hostile or judgmental environment.

In order to truly choose grace over judgment, it is essential that we also extend this kindness and understanding towards ourselves. Often, we are our harshest critics, constantly judging ourselves for our perceived flaws or mistakes. However, by practicing self-compassion and treating ourselves with grace, we can break free from the cycle of self-judgment and cultivate a healthier relationship with ourselves.

Choosing grace over judgment is not always easy. It requires conscious effort and a willingness to let go of our own biases and preconceived notions. However, the rewards are immense – deeper connections with others, increased empathy, and a more harmonious world.

As we continue on our journey of self-awareness and personal growth, let us remember the power of choosing grace over judgment. By embracing kindness and understanding in our interactions with others – as well as towards ourselves – we can create a more compassionate society where acceptance and empathy thrive.

In the next chapter, we will explore the language of self-love and how transforming negative self-talk can contribute to cultivating grace over judgment in our own lives.

CHAPTER 6: THE LANGUAGE OF SELF-LOVE: TRANSFORMING NEGATIVE SELF-TALK

In this chapter, we delve into the power of self-talk and its impact on our self-perception. We will explore how negative self-talk patterns can hinder our growth and prevent us from embracing self-love. By identifying these patterns, we can take steps to transform them into affirmations and positive language, paving the way for a more compassionate relationship with ourselves.

Our inner dialogue is like a constant stream of thoughts that shape our perception of ourselves and the world around us. Unfortunately, many of us have developed negative self-talk patterns over time, rooted in fear, insecurities, or past experiences. This internal criticism not only affects our confidence but also perpetuates a cycle of judgment towards ourselves.

To begin transforming negative self-talk, it is essential to first become aware of the specific language we use when speaking to ourselves. Pay attention to the words you choose and the tone in which you address yourself. Are they kind and supportive? Or do they reflect harsh judgment and criticism?

Once identified, challenge these negative thoughts by replacing them with affirmations or positive language that promotes self-acceptance and love. For example, if you catch yourself thinking, "I'm so stupid for making that mistake," replace it with "Mistakes happen; I am learning and growing from this experience."

Remember that changing ingrained thought patterns takes time and practice. Be patient with yourself as you navigate this process of transformation. Celebrate small victories along the way and remind yourself that every effort counts towards cultivating a more loving relationship with yourself.

Another helpful strategy is surrounding yourself with positive influences such as uplifting books, podcasts, or affirmations that reinforce self-love. These resources can serve as reminders to counteract any negative thoughts that may arise throughout your day.

Additionally, practicing mindfulness can greatly assist in transforming negative self-talk into positive affirmations. Mindfulness involves observing your thoughts without judgment and redirecting them towards more compassionate and empowering narratives. By anchoring yourself in the present moment, you create an opportunity to challenge negative self-talk patterns and replace them with kinder, more supportive thoughts.

It's important to note that transforming negative self-talk is not about denying or suppressing our emotions. Instead, it's about acknowledging our vulnerabilities and responding to ourselves with understanding and empathy. By accepting our imperfections and treating ourselves with compassion, we pave the way for growth, healing, and a deeper connection with our true selves.

As we continue on this journey of self-love through transforming our language of self-talk, we may encounter setbacks or moments when old patterns resurface. It's crucial to remember that these moments do not define us but rather provide opportunities for further growth.

The language we use towards ourselves is a powerful tool that can either uplift or discourage us. By consciously choosing words that promote self-acceptance, forgiveness, and love, we create space for personal transformation. We become the authors of our own stories – stories filled with kindness, understanding, and resilience.

Transforming negative self-talk into positive affirmations is a vital step in cultivating self-love. By becoming aware of our inner dialogue and challenging negative thought patterns with kindness and compassion, we can break free from the cycle of judgment towards ourselves. Let us embrace this journey of transformation as we rewrite the narrative within us - one filled with love, acceptance, and unwavering belief in our inherent worthiness.

CHAPTER 7: CULTIVATING EMPATHY: STEPPING INTO OTHERS' SHOES

In this final chapter of "Understanding They Aren't Judging you, they are judging themselves," we delve into the transformative power of empathy. We explore how stepping into the shoes of others allows us to deepen our understanding and connection with those around us. By cultivating empathy, we can not only break free from judgment but also foster harmonious and compassionate relationships.

Empathy is often misunderstood as merely sympathizing or feeling sorry for someone. However, true empathy goes beyond that; it involves actively putting ourselves in another person's position and seeking to understand their emotions, thoughts, and experiences without judgment. It requires openness, curiosity, and a genuine desire to connect on a deeper level.

To develop empathy, we must first acknowledge our own biases and prejudices that hinder our ability to truly understand others. We all carry subconscious beliefs shaped by our upbringing, culture, and personal experiences. These beliefs can create barriers between ourselves and others if left unexamined.

Therefore, self-awareness is crucial in unearthing these biases and allowing us to approach situations with an open mind.

One effective way to cultivate empathy is through active listening. When engaging in conversation with someone else—whether a friend or a stranger—practice being fully present and attentive. Set aside your own preconceived notions or desire to respond immediately, instead focus on truly hearing the other person's words without interruption or judgment. By doing so, you create a safe space for them to express themselves openly while showing them respect and validation.

Another powerful tool for developing empathy is practicing perspective-taking. This involves imagining yourself in another person's situation by considering their background, experiences, values, and emotions. It requires setting aside your own biases temporarily to gain insight into their worldviews fully.

To enhance perspective-taking skills further, engage in diverse experiences intentionally. Seek out opportunities to interact with people from different cultures, backgrounds, and perspectives. This exposure broadens your understanding of the world and challenges any limited beliefs you may hold.

Empathy also requires the ability to recognize and manage your own emotions effectively. By developing emotional intelligence, you become better equipped to empathize with others' emotions without becoming overwhelmed by them. This self-regulation allows you to be present for others while maintaining healthy boundaries and taking care of your own well-being.

In our fast-paced society, it is easy to get caught up in our own lives and neglect the needs of those around us. However, fostering empathy means actively making an effort to connect with others on a deeper level. Simple acts of kindness can go a long way in building empathy within ourselves and inspiring it in others.

In addition to personal relationships, cultivating empathy extends into our communities as well. It involves recognizing systemic injustices and advocating for change that benefits all individuals regardless of their background or circumstances. Through collective empathy, we strive for a more inclusive society where everyone feels seen, heard, and valued.

As we conclude this book on understanding judgment from others as a reflection of their internal struggles rather than a personal attack on ourselves, let us remember that empathy is an ongoing practice. It requires continuous self-reflection, open-mindedness, and genuine curiosity about the experiences of those around us.

By embracing empathy as a guiding principle in our interactions with others, we not only break free from the cycle of judgment but also cultivate deep connections based on mutual understanding and compassion. Let us step into each other's shoes with grace and kindness as we navigate this complex journey called life together.

May this book serve as a reminder that true understanding begins within ourselves—by nurturing self-awareness—and radiates outward through empathy towards others. As we embrace these principles in our daily lives, we contribute to building a more compassionate world—one where judgment is replaced by understanding and acceptance.

Remember: They aren't judging you; they are judging themselves. Let empathy be our guiding light on this transformative journey of self-discovery and connection.

CHAPTER 8: CULTIVATING MINDFULNESS AND SELF-REFLECTION

In this chapter, we will delve into the transformative power of mindfulness and self-reflection. By utilizing these practices, we can develop a deeper understanding of ourselves and others. Through clarity and intention, we can let go of judgments and cultivate empathy.

Section 1: The Power of Mindfulness

Mindfulness is the practice of being fully present in the moment without judgment. It allows us to observe our thoughts, emotions, and sensations with curiosity rather than reacting impulsively. By cultivating mindfulness, we can stay grounded in self-awareness and navigate life's challenges with grace.

Subsection 1.1: Staying Grounded in Self-Awareness

When we are mindful, we are better able to recognize our patterns of thinking, feeling, and behaving. We become aware of our triggers that lead to judgment or criticism. By staying grounded in self-awareness, we can catch ourselves before falling into the trap of judging others.

Subsection 1.2: Observing Thoughts and Emotions

Through mindfulness practices such as meditation or deep breathing exercises, we learn to observe our thoughts and emotions without getting entangled in them. This allows us to gain clarity about what is truly happening within us before projecting it onto others.

Section 2: The Art of Self-Reflection

Self-reflection is a powerful tool for personal growth and understanding. It involves taking the time to examine our thoughts, motivations, beliefs, and actions with honesty and compassion.

Subsection 2.1: Creating Space for Reflection

In today's fast-paced world, it is easy to get caught up in the busyness of life without taking time for introspection. However, by intentionally creating space for reflection - whether through journaling or quiet contemplation - we open ourselves up to deeper insights about ourselves.

Subsection 2.2: Uncovering Our Inner Landscape

Self-reflection allows us to delve into the depths of our inner landscape. We explore our fears, insecurities, and past experiences that shape our judgments. By shining a light on these aspects of ourselves, we can begin to heal and grow.

Section 3: Letting Go of Judgments

As we cultivate mindfulness and engage in self-reflection, we gain a deeper understanding that judgments stem from our own insecurities and biases. By letting go of judgments, we create space for empathy and compassion towards ourselves and others.

Subsection 3.1: Recognizing the Source of Judgments

Through self-reflection, we can uncover the root causes of our judgments. We may realize that they originate from societal conditioning or unresolved personal issues. By recognizing the source, we can detach ourselves from these judgments.

Subsection 3.2: Cultivating Empathy and Compassion

With mindfulness and self-reflection as our allies, we can develop empathy towards others' struggles. We understand that everyone is navigating their own challenges and judging themselves just as harshly as they judge us. Compassion becomes a natural response instead of judgment.

Conclusion:

Mindfulness and self-reflection are powerful practices that enable us to understand that when others judge us, it is not about us but rather about their own internal struggles. By staying grounded in self-awareness, observing our thoughts without judgment, creating space for reflection, uncovering our inner landscape with honesty, and letting go of judgments through empathy and compassion - we embark on a transformative journey towards understanding ourselves better while fostering deep connections with those around us.

CHAPTER 9: THE JOURNEY OF SELF-DISCOVERY

As we continue on our journey towards self-understanding and personal growth, it becomes crucial to engage in activities that allow us to uncover our hidden beliefs and patterns. It is through this process of self-discovery that we can begin to unravel the layers of conditioning and gain a deeper understanding of ourselves.

Self-discovery is not a one-time event; rather, it is an ongoing commitment to personal growth and development. It requires us to be open and curious, willing to explore the depths of our being. By engaging in various activities, we can gain insights into who we truly are and shed light on the unconscious patterns that shape our thoughts, feelings, and behaviors.

One powerful tool for self-discovery is journaling. Through writing down our thoughts, emotions, dreams, and aspirations, we create a space for reflection and introspection. Journaling allows us to express ourselves freely without judgment or constraint. As we pour out our innermost thoughts onto paper, patterns begin to emerge - recurring themes that provide clues about our deepest desires and fears.

Another valuable activity for self-discovery is meditation. By sitting in silence and observing our thoughts with non-judgmental awareness, we can uncover the underlying beliefs that drive our actions. Meditation teaches us how to detach from the constant chatter of the mind and tap into a deeper level of consciousness where profound insights reside.

Engaging in artistic endeavors such as painting or sculpting can also unlock hidden aspects of ourselves. When we allow creativity to flow through us, unfiltered by societal expectations or judgments, we tap into a wellspring of authenticity. Artistic expression invites us to explore different facets of our identity while providing an outlet for emotions that may otherwise remain buried.

Furthermore, seeking guidance from mentors or therapists can facilitate the process of self-discovery. These individuals possess wisdom gained through their own journeys and can offer valuable insights into patterns that may be invisible to us. By listening to their perspectives and sharing our experiences, we gain new perspectives and expand our understanding of ourselves.

It is crucial to remember that self-discovery is not a linear path. It is filled with twists and turns, moments of clarity, and periods of confusion. Embracing the journey requires patience and self-compassion. We must allow ourselves the space to make mistakes, learn from them, and grow.

As we delve deeper into the realm of self-discovery, we may encounter resistance - both internal and external. Our own fears and insecurities can manifest as self-doubt or feelings of unworthiness. The judgments we face from others can act as mirrors reflecting back our own inner critic.

In these moments, it is essential to remind ourselves that they are not judging us but rather judging themselves through their own lens of perception. Our journey towards self-discovery is unique to us; others may not understand or resonate with it fully. It is important to stay true to ourselves despite external opinions or criticism.

By embracing this perspective, we can free ourselves from the burden of seeking validation from others. We realize that their judgments stem from their own insecurities and limitations; they do not define who we are or what we are capable of achieving.

The path towards self-discovery is a courageous one - a journey that requires vulnerability, introspection, and a willingness to confront our deepest truths. As we engage in activities that uncover hidden beliefs and patterns while committing ourselves to ongoing personal growth, we pave the way for profound transformation.

In the next chapter, we will explore how embracing vulnerability can deepen our connection with others while fostering authenticity within ourselves. Through understanding that vulnerability is not weakness but rather a strength born out of courage, we can cultivate meaningful relationships based on openness and acceptance.

CHAPTER 10: EMBRACING IMPERFECTION

As we journey through life, it becomes evident that perfection is an elusive and unattainable concept. Yet, our society constantly bombards us with images of flawlessness and ideals that seem unattainable. It is in this culture of perfectionism that we find ourselves constantly striving to measure up, to be better, and to avoid judgment from others.

But what if I were to tell you that those judgments are not about you at all? That they are merely reflections of the insecurities and self-doubts harbored by others. This chapter aims to explore the idea of radical acceptance – the ability to embrace imperfection as a part of the human experience.

To truly understand radical acceptance, we must first delve into its essence – accepting ourselves without judgment. Our worth as individuals is not determined by our flaws or mistakes but rather by our ability to acknowledge them with compassion and kindness. It is through this lens of self-acceptance that we can extend the same grace towards others.

In a world obsessed with judgment and comparison, embracing imperfection may seem like a radical notion. However, it is precisely in our imperfections where true beauty lies. Each scar tells a story; each mistake offers an opportunity for growth. It is only when we strip away the layers of judgment that we can fully appreciate the uniqueness and authenticity within ourselves and others.

Radical acceptance requires us to let go of societal expectations and redefine our own standards of success and happiness. By releasing ourselves from the constant pursuit of perfection, we open up space for self-discovery, exploration, and genuine connections with those around us.

Imagine a world where society valued vulnerability over invulnerability – where sharing our struggles became an act of courage rather than weakness. In such a world, judgments would dissipate as empathy takes its place. We would no longer fear being judged because we would recognize that those judgments stem from the insecurities and self-criticism of others.

To practice radical acceptance, we must first acknowledge our own self-judgments. Take a moment to reflect on the ways in which you criticize yourself – the harsh words, the unattainable expectations, and the relentless pursuit of perfection. By shining a light on these internal judgments, we can begin to challenge their validity and replace them with self-compassion.

It is important to remember that radical acceptance does not mean complacency or resignation. Rather, it is an active choice to embrace our imperfections while striving for personal growth. It is about recognizing that life is messy, and that's okay. It's about accepting that failure is not a reflection of our worth but rather an opportunity for learning and resilience.

As we cultivate radical acceptance within ourselves, we also extend this compassion towards others. We become less inclined to judge those around us because we understand that their actions are often driven by their own struggles and insecurities. We realize that by judging others, we perpetuate a cycle of negativity and disconnection.

Embracing imperfection through radical acceptance is not only liberating but also transformative. It allows us to break free from the constraints of judgment and comparison, offering us an opportunity to live authentically and wholeheartedly. By choosing self-acceptance over self-judgment and extending empathy towards others, we foster a culture of compassion where true connection can thrive.

So let us release ourselves from the burden of perfectionism and embark on a journey towards radical acceptance – embracing imperfection as an integral part of who we are as human beings. For in doing so, we not only find peace within ourselves but also create a world where judgments are replaced with understanding and love.

CHAPTER 11: THE COURAGE TO BE VULNERABLE

In the journey of understanding ourselves and others, one topic that often arises is vulnerability. It is a concept that can evoke fear, discomfort, and uncertainty in many individuals. However, as we delve deeper into the realm of vulnerability, we come to realize that it holds immense power and potential for growth and connection.

Stepping out of our comfort zones to embrace vulnerability takes great courage. It requires us to let go of our shields and masks, allowing ourselves to be seen in our most raw and authentic state. In doing so, we expose ourselves to the possibility of judgment and rejection. Yet, it is precisely through this exposure that we can find true connection with others.

When we choose vulnerability over self-protection, we create an environment where authenticity thrives. We give others permission to be vulnerable themselves by leading by example. This act of courage paves the way for deeper connections built on trust and empathy.

Often, our fear of judgment stems from a belief that others are constantly scrutinizing us. We convince ourselves that they are judging every move we make or every word we say. However, what if I told you that most judgments stem from people's own insecurities rather than a genuine evaluation of us?

It may seem counterintuitive at first glance but think about it for a moment - why would someone who feels secure within themselves waste their time judging others? In reality, when people judge us harshly or unfairly criticize our actions or choices, they are projecting their own struggles onto us.

Understanding this truth can be liberating. It allows us to detach from the opinions and judgments of others because deep down inside; we know they aren't truly evaluating us but rather grappling with their own demons.

By embracing vulnerability instead of fearing judgment, not only do we free ourselves from unnecessary anxiety but also open up opportunities for compassion towards those who judge us harshly. We begin to see them not as adversaries but as individuals who are struggling within themselves. This realization can help us respond with empathy instead of defensiveness, fostering understanding and connection.

In our quest for self-discovery and growth, vulnerability becomes an essential tool. It is through exposing our vulnerabilities that we invite others to connect with us on a deeper level. In sharing our fears, insecurities, and struggles, we create an environment where others feel safe enough to do the same.

The courage to be vulnerable extends beyond personal relationships; it also impacts professional settings. When we allow ourselves to be vulnerable at work, we foster an environment of trust and collaboration. By acknowledging our limitations and seeking help when needed, we show strength rather than weakness.

Furthermore, vulnerability allows for creativity and innovation to flourish. When we are open to sharing imperfect ideas or taking risks without the fear of judgment or failure, we often reach breakthroughs that would have otherwise remained hidden in the shadows of self-protection.

So how can we cultivate the courage to be vulnerable? It starts with embracing imperfection and accepting that vulnerability is not a sign of weakness but rather a testament to our authenticity and humanity. We must let go of unrealistic expectations placed upon ourselves by society or even by ourselves.

Practicing self-compassion is crucial in this journey. Treating ourselves with kindness when facing setbacks or moments of vulnerability allows us to build resilience and continue growing despite any judgments or criticisms that come our way.

As we navigate through life's ups and downs, it is important for us all to remember that they aren't judging us; they are judging themselves. By embracing vulnerability with courage and openness, not only do we liberate ourselves from fear but also invite others into a world where genuine connections thrive - a world where understanding replaces judgment.

CHAPTER 12: THE COURAGE IN BEING VULNERABLE

The room was hushed as Sarah stood before a crowd of eager listeners. Her heart pounded in her chest; her palms sweaty with nervous anticipation. Speaking in public had always been a daunting task for her, but today she had chosen to step out of her comfort zone and embrace vulnerability.

In this chapter, we will explore the transformative power of vulnerability and how it allows us to build authentic connections through courage and openness.

Vulnerability is often misunderstood as weakness. Society has conditioned us to believe that showing our true selves, raw and unfiltered, leaves us open to judgment and rejection. However, the truth is that vulnerability takes immense strength. It requires us to confront our fears head-on and expose our innermost thoughts and emotions without reservation.

Sarah's journey towards embracing vulnerability began when she realized that by hiding behind a façade of perfectionism, she was depriving herself of genuine connections with others. She had always feared being judged or criticized for her imperfections. But deep down, she knew that people were not judging her; they were merely judging themselves through the lens of their own insecurities.

As Sarah took the microphone in hand, she felt a surge of courage coursing through her veins. She shared personal stories from her life - tales of failure, heartbreak, and moments when she felt most vulnerable. The audience listened intently as Sarah bared her soul before them.

She explained how vulnerability allows us to connect on a deeper level with others because it creates an atmosphere where authenticity thrives. When we let go of the need for perfectionism or pretense, we invite others to do the same. By sharing our vulnerabilities openly, we give permission for others to do the same without fear or judgment.

Sarah recounted an incident from earlier in the day when one brave individual approached her after her talk with tears streaming down their faces. They thanked Sarah for sharing her vulnerabilities because it gave them the courage to confront their own. In that moment, Sarah realized the immense power of vulnerability to inspire and uplift others.

Being vulnerable also allows us to cultivate empathy and compassion. When we expose our true selves, flaws and all, we create an environment where others feel safe to do the same. It is through this shared vulnerability that we can truly understand one another's pain, struggles, and triumphs.

Sarah shared a quote from Brené Brown: "Vulnerability is not winning or losing; it's having the courage to show up and be seen when we have no control over the outcome." This resonated deeply with her audience as they reflected on their own experiences of vulnerability.

To be vulnerable requires self-acceptance and self-love. It demands that we embrace our imperfections and recognize that they are an integral part of our unique journey. By accepting ourselves fully, we give others permission to accept themselves as well.

As Sarah concluded her talk, there was a collective sense of empowerment in the room. The audience had witnessed firsthand the transformative power of vulnerability - how it had the ability to mend broken hearts, forge new connections, and ignite personal growth.

In this chapter, we have explored how embracing vulnerability takes immense courage but ultimately leads us towards authentic connections with others. By shedding our masks of perfectionism and allowing ourselves to be seen for who we truly are, we create an environment where empathy flourishes.

Sarah's journey towards embracing vulnerability was just one example among many. Each person has their own unique path towards finding the courage to be vulnerable. And by doing so, they discover a world filled with deeper connections, understanding, acceptance - both for themselves and for others.

As you reflect upon your own experiences with vulnerability thus far in your life journey, consider what walls you may still have up preventing you from fully embracing your authentic self. Remember that true strength lies not in hiding our vulnerabilities but in having the courage to embrace them.

CHAPTER 13: CULTIVATING SELF-COMPASSION

In the journey of understanding and embracing our authentic selves, it is crucial to cultivate a sense of compassion and kindness towards ourselves. Often, we find ourselves being overly critical and judgmental of our own actions and decisions. This chapter explores the significance of self-compassion and how practicing self-care can transform our relationship with ourselves.

We live in a world that constantly bombards us with expectations, standards, and comparisons. It is easy to fall into the trap of self-judgment when we perceive ourselves as falling short or not meeting these external ideals. However, what we often fail to realize is that this judgment stems from our own insecurities and struggles.

Practicing self-compassion begins with acknowledging that we are human beings who are imperfect by nature. We all make mistakes, experience failures, and have moments when we feel vulnerable or uncertain. Instead of berating ourselves for these perceived flaws or shortcomings, it is essential to treat ourselves with kindness and understanding.

One powerful way to cultivate self-compassion is through acts of self-care. Just as we would extend love and care towards a dear friend or family member in need, we should offer the same level of empathy towards ourselves. Taking time for activities that bring us joy, relaxation, or rejuvenation allows us to recharge both physically and emotionally.

Self-care can take various forms depending on individual preferences - it could involve indulging in a bubble bath after a long day at work; taking a leisurely walk in nature; meditating; engaging in creative pursuits such as painting or writing; or simply spending quality time alone doing something that brings solace.

Engaging in regular self-care not only nurtures our well-being but also sends a powerful message to our subconscious mind that we value ourselves enough to prioritize our needs. It reinforces the belief that even amidst life's demands and responsibilities, taking care of oneself is not a luxury but a necessity.

However, self-compassion goes beyond the external acts of self-care. It involves cultivating an inner dialogue that is supportive and understanding. Often, our internal voice can be harsh and critical, exacerbating our insecurities and fears. By consciously shifting this narrative to one of self-compassion and acceptance, we can transform our relationship with ourselves.

Imagine a dear friend confiding in you about their struggles or failures. Would you respond with judgment and criticism? Most likely not. Instead, you would offer words of encouragement, understanding, and support. Similarly, when we encounter challenges or setbacks in our own lives, it is crucial to adopt the same compassionate approach towards ourselves.

Practicing self-compassion does not mean disregarding personal growth or accountability for our actions. It simply means acknowledging that mistakes are opportunities for learning rather than reasons for self-condemnation. By embracing self-compassion as an integral part of our journey towards authenticity, we create a safe space within ourselves to explore, grow, and evolve.

Cultivating self-compassion is paramount in understanding that judgment from others often stems from their own insecurities rather than any inherent flaw within us. By practicing acts of self-care and adopting an inner dialogue rooted in kindness and empathy, we can transform how we perceive ourselves and navigate through life's challenges with greater resilience.

Remember that each step on this journey towards authenticity requires patience and effort; it is okay to stumble along the way. Let go of the need for perfectionism and embrace the beautiful messiness that comes with being human. They aren't judging you; they are judging themselves - just as you once did before embarking on this transformative path of self-discovery.

So be gentle with yourself as you navigate through life's uncertainties; treat yourself with the love and compassion that every soul deserves. In doing so, you will uncover a profound sense of inner peace, acceptance, and the courage to shine your light unapologetically in this world.

CHAPTER 14: EMBRACING IMPERFECTION

As human beings, we often find ourselves trapped in the never-ending pursuit of perfection. We strive to achieve flawless appearances, impeccable achievements, and faultless relationships. But in this relentless quest for perfection, we fail to realize that it is a futile endeavor. Perfection is an illusion, a mirage that forever eludes our grasp.

In this chapter, we will explore the concept of letting go of control and embracing the beauty of imperfection. It is through acknowledging our own imperfections and accepting them that we can find true freedom and inner peace.

Our desire for control stems from a deep-seated fear of the unknown. We mistakenly believe that if we can control every aspect of our lives, everything will fall into place perfectly. However, life rarely unfolds according to our plans. It is unpredictable and messy, filled with unexpected twists and turns.

Acknowledging the futility of seeking perfection in ourselves and others is the first step towards liberation. We must let go of the need to constantly compare ourselves to others or measure up to unattainable standards set by society. Instead, we should focus on self-acceptance and self-love.

Sarah's journey serves as an example of how surrendering control can lead to personal growth and transformation. Like many others, Sarah was plagued by self-doubt and an insatiable desire for perfection. She believed that if she could just control every aspect of her life - her appearance, her career, her relationships - she would finally be happy.

But as Sarah soon discovered through a series of setbacks and disappointments, her pursuit of perfection only brought her anxiety and dissatisfaction. It was when she hit rock bottom that she realized something profound - true happiness lies not in controlling every aspect of one's life but in embracing imperfection.

Through therapy sessions with Dr. Adams, Sarah learned valuable lessons about self-compassion and acceptance. She discovered that her worth as a person was not determined by external achievements or appearances but by the love and kindness, she showed herself.

One particular exercise that Dr. Adams assigned to Sarah proved to be a turning point in her journey towards self-acceptance. She was asked to write down all the qualities she admired in others, focusing on their imperfections rather than their perfections. This exercise helped Sarah shift her perspective and realize that imperfections are what make us unique and beautiful.

By surrendering control, Sarah opened herself up to new possibilities and experiences. She began accepting invitations from friends without meticulously planning every detail, allowing herself to enjoy spontaneous moments of joy and laughter. She also started experimenting with hobbies she had previously dismissed as "not good enough," realizing that it was the process of trying and learning that brought her fulfillment, not the end result.

Sarah's newfound embrace of imperfection extended beyond herself to how she viewed others as well. Rather than judging people based on surface-level appearances or achievements, she started seeing them as complex individuals with their own struggles and insecurities.

The fundamental truth is this: when we judge others harshly, we are not truly judging them; we are judging ourselves. Our judgments reflect our own deep-rooted insecurities and fears. By acknowledging our own imperfections, we can develop empathy and compassion for others who are also navigating life's uncertainties.

Letting go of control is no easy feat; it requires courage and vulnerability. But it is through this surrender that we find liberation from the shackles of perfectionism. Embracing imperfection allows us to live authentically, celebrating our strengths while accepting our weaknesses.

Chapter 14 explores the transformative power of letting go of control and embracing imperfection. Through Sarah's journey towards self-acceptance, we learn that true happiness lies not in seeking perfection but in embracing our flaws with compassion and love. By shifting our perspective and acknowledging the futility of seeking perfection, we can experience a profound sense of freedom and inner peace.

CHAPTER 15: THE HEALING POWER OF FORGIVENESS

In the journey of understanding that they aren't judging you, they are judging themselves, one of the most transformative and liberating practices we can embrace is the power of forgiveness. It is through forgiveness that we can heal emotional wounds and transform past hurts into opportunities for growth and wisdom.

Forgiveness is not about condoning or excusing the actions of others. It is not about forgetting or pretending that the pain inflicted upon us didn't happen. Rather, forgiveness is a deliberate choice to release ourselves from the grip of resentment and anger, allowing us to find peace within ourselves.

When we hold onto grudges and refuse to forgive, it's like carrying a heavy burden on our shoulders. The weight of anger and bitterness weighs us down, preventing us from moving forward in life. But when we choose to forgive, we unburden ourselves from this weight and create space for healing.

The practice of forgiveness starts with acknowledging our pain and allowing ourselves to feel it fully. It requires us to confront our emotions head-on rather than suppressing them. By doing so, we honor our own experiences while also recognizing that holding onto negative emotions will only prolong our suffering.

Once we have acknowledged our pain, it becomes essential to cultivate empathy towards those who have hurt us. This doesn't mean justifying their actions or minimizing the impact they had on our lives; rather, it means trying to understand their perspective and recognizing that they too might be trapped in their own cycle of pain.

In understanding that they aren't judging you but rather judging themselves, we begin to see how their actions might stem from their own insecurities or unresolved traumas. This realization allows us to shift away from taking things personally and opens up space for compassion towards both ourselves and others.

One powerful tool in the process of forgiveness is writing a letter addressed directly to those who have caused us harm. Pouring out our feelings onto paper can be incredibly cathartic, allowing us to express our pain and anger in a safe and controlled manner. While we may never send these letters, the act of writing them helps us release the emotional charge associated with the past events.

As we navigate the path of forgiveness, it is important to remember that it is not a linear process. Healing takes time, and there will be moments when old wounds resurface, triggering feelings of anger and resentment. However, each time we choose forgiveness over bitterness, we strengthen our emotional resilience and move closer towards true healing.

Forgiving ourselves is also an integral part of this process. Often, we hold onto guilt and self-blame for mistakes made or perceived shortcomings. But just as we extend compassion towards others in their journey of self-judgment, it is crucial to offer the same kindness to ourselves.

Self-forgiveness means acknowledging our imperfections and understanding that growth comes through learning from our mistakes rather than dwelling on them. It involves making peace with our past choices and embracing the possibility of personal growth going forward.

The healing power of forgiveness extends beyond ourselves; it ripples out into all areas of our lives. As we let go of grudges and resentments, we create space for healthier relationships based on empathy and understanding. We free ourselves from toxic patterns that keep us stuck in cycles of pain.

Understanding that they aren't judging you but rather judging themselves opens up a world where forgiveness becomes a catalyst for profound healing. Through forgiveness, we release ourselves from the burden of resentment and anger while cultivating empathy towards both ourselves and others. It is through this practice that wounds transform into opportunities for growth and wisdom—a testament to the transformative power inherent within each one of us on this journey called life.

CHAPTER 16: THE POWER OF GRATITUDE

As we navigate through the complexities of life, it is easy to become consumed by our own insecurities and fears. We often find ourselves caught in a web of self-doubt, constantly wondering what others think of us. But what if I told you that their judgment has little to do with us and everything to do with themselves?

In this chapter, we will explore the transformative power of gratitude and how it can help us break free from the shackles of judgment. By cultivating a daily habit of gratitude, we can shift our focus towards positivity and find joy and fulfillment in even the simplest moments of life.

Practicing gratitude is not just about saying "thank you" when someone does something nice for us; it goes much deeper than that. It involves actively seeking out moments of appreciation throughout our day, no matter how small or insignificant they may seem.

Imagine waking up every morning with a sense of anticipation, eagerly awaiting the beautiful moments that lie ahead. It could be as simple as savoring your first sip of coffee or feeling the warmth of sunlight on your face during a morning walk. By consciously acknowledging these moments and expressing gratitude for them, we open ourselves up to a world filled with wonder and beauty.

One way to cultivate gratitude is by keeping a gratitude journal. Each evening before bed, take a few minutes to reflect on your day and write down three things you are grateful for. These could be experiences, people, or even personal qualities that you appreciate about yourself.

As you embark on this journey towards cultivating gratitude, you may notice subtle shifts in your mindset. The more you focus on the positives in your life, the less attention you give to negative judgments from others. You begin to realize that their opinions are merely reflections of their own insecurities and struggles.

It's important to remember that everyone has their own battles they are fighting behind closed doors. The judgments they cast upon us are often projections of their own self-doubt and fear. By understanding this, we can free ourselves from the burden of their judgment and find compassion instead.

In moments when you feel judged, take a step back and remind yourself of your own worth. Recognize that you are on a unique journey filled with ups and downs, just like everyone else. Embrace the lessons you have learned along the way and celebrate your growth.

Gratitude also has the power to enhance our relationships with others. When we express genuine appreciation for those around us, we strengthen the bonds that tie us together. Take a moment each day to let someone know how grateful you are for their presence in your life. It could be a heartfelt note, a kind gesture, or simply saying "thank you" with sincerity.

As we practice gratitude daily, not only do we transform our own lives but also create a ripple effect that touches those around us. Our positive energy becomes contagious, inspiring others to shift their focus towards gratitude as well.

So let us embark on this journey of cultivating gratitude together - one moment at a time. As we learn to appreciate even the smallest blessings in our lives, we empower ourselves to rise above judgment and embrace a life filled with joy and fulfillment.

Remember, they aren't judging you; they are judging themselves. So release yourself from their judgments and embrace the power of gratitude – for it is through grateful hearts that true freedom is found.

CHAPTER 17: EMBRACING SELF-COMPASSION

As human beings, we often find it easier to extend kindness and compassion to others rather than ourselves. We are quick to offer a helping hand or a comforting word to those around us, but when it comes to our own struggles and shortcomings, we can be incredibly harsh and unforgiving. In this chapter, we will explore the concept of self-compassion and how it can transform our relationship with ourselves.

Imagine a close friend coming to you with tears in their eyes, burdened by the weight of their mistakes. How would you respond? Chances are, you would offer them words of comfort and reassurance. You would remind them that everyone makes mistakes and that they are still worthy of love and acceptance. Now, think about how you would react if you were the one facing those same challenges.

Often, when faced with our own failures or perceived inadequacies, we become our harshest critics. We berate ourselves for not being good enough or for making mistakes. We compare ourselves unfavorably to others who seem to have it all figured out. This self-judgment only serves to deepen our wounds and hinder our growth.

But what if we could learn to treat ourselves with the same kindness and compassion that we extend towards others? What if instead of beating ourselves up over every misstep, we offered understanding and forgiveness? This is where self-compassion comes in.

Self-compassion is about recognizing that as human beings, we are inherently flawed. It is acknowledging that making mistakes is part of the learning process and does not diminish our worthiness as individuals. It involves treating ourselves with kindness rather than criticism when faced with challenges or setbacks.

One powerful way to cultivate self-compassion is through a practice known as loving-kindness meditation. This practice involves directing positive intentions towards yourself as well as others in order to cultivate feelings of compassion and empathy. By repeating phrases such as "May I be happy, may I be healthy, may I live with ease," you are sending love and kindness to yourself.

Another important aspect of self-compassion is learning to embrace our emotional wounds. Just as physical wounds require care and attention to heal, so do our emotional scars. Instead of avoiding or suppressing painful emotions, we can learn to hold space for them with kindness and understanding. This process allows us to acknowledge our pain without judgment, leading to healing and growth.

It's important to remember that self-compassion is not about making excuses for ourselves or shying away from responsibility. It is about acknowledging our humanity and treating ourselves with the same compassion we would offer a loved one in need. By doing so, we create a foundation of self-love that enables us to navigate life's challenges with greater resilience and grace.

Practicing self-compassion can feel uncomfortable at first, especially if you have spent years engaging in self-criticism and judgment. However, like any skill, it can be cultivated with time and practice. Start by simply noticing the ways in which you speak to yourself internally. Are your words kind and supportive or critical and harsh? Begin replacing negative self-talk with words of encouragement and understanding.

Remember that embracing self-compassion is not a sign of weakness but rather an act of strength. It takes courage to face our vulnerabilities head-on without judgment or shame. As you embark on this journey towards greater self-compassion, be patient with yourself. Rome wasn't built in a day, and neither will your capacity for self-love.

By embracing self-compassion we open ourselves up to a world of healing possibilities. We learn that we are worthy of love and acceptance regardless of our flaws or mistakes. Through practices such as loving-kindness meditation and holding space for our emotional wounds, we cultivate a deep sense of self-love and understanding. So, let us embark on this journey together, hand in hand with self-compassion as our guide.

CHAPTER 18: THE POWER OF BOUNDARIES

In this chapter, we will explore the role of boundaries in our lives and how they can protect us from toxic influences. Boundaries are essential for maintaining our emotional well-being and honoring our own needs. By establishing healthy boundaries, we can create a safe space where we feel respected and valued.

We live in a world filled with various interactions and relationships. Some of these interactions can be positive and uplifting, while others may drain us emotionally or even harm us. It is crucial to recognize that we have the power to set boundaries that safeguard our mental health.

Boundaries act as invisible lines that define what is acceptable and what is not in our relationships. They serve as guidelines for how others should treat us, ensuring that we are treated with respect and dignity. Establishing healthy boundaries is an act of self-love, a way to prioritize our well-being without feeling guilty or selfish.

Toxic influences can come in many forms - from demanding friends who constantly take advantage of our kindness to family members who disregard our feelings and boundaries. Without clear boundaries, we risk becoming entangled in unhealthy dynamics that drain us emotionally. However, by asserting ourselves through the establishment of firm limits, we take control over these situations.

Recognizing the importance of honoring your own needs is fundamental when setting boundaries. It requires acknowledging that your emotions matter and deserve validation. By establishing clear limits on what you will tolerate or accept from others, you send a powerful message about your self-worth.

Boundaries provide structure within relationships; they establish expectations for behavior while creating a sense of safety for all parties involved. When communicated effectively, boundaries help foster healthier connections built on mutual respect and understanding.

It's important to remember that setting boundaries does not mean cutting people off or shutting them out completely; rather it involves creating space for yourself within relationships where you feel comfortable expressing your needs openly without fear of judgment or retribution.

Boundaries can be physical, emotional, or even intellectual. Physical boundaries involve personal space and touch, while emotional boundaries relate to your feelings and emotions. Intellectual boundaries pertain to your thoughts, beliefs, and opinions. Each of these areas requires attention and protection in order for us to maintain a healthy sense of self.

Practicing assertiveness is key when establishing boundaries. It involves communicating our needs clearly and respectfully while also listening to the needs of others. Assertive communication allows us to express ourselves authentically without resorting to aggression or passivity.

Remember that setting boundaries may initially be challenging, especially if you have been conditioned to prioritize the needs of others over your own. It takes courage and self-awareness to recognize that you deserve respect and consideration just as much as anyone else.

As you embark on this journey of boundary-setting, it's important to be patient with yourself. Start small by identifying areas where you feel your boundaries are being crossed or neglected. Reflect on what makes you uncomfortable or triggered in those situations and consider what limits would help protect your emotional well-being.

Communicate your boundaries clearly but kindly with those around you. Remember that not everyone may understand or respect them immediately; however, by consistently enforcing your boundaries with compassion, people will come to understand what is acceptable behavior in their interactions with you.

Establishing healthy boundaries is crucial for safeguarding our well-being and maintaining positive relationships. By setting clear limits on how we allow others to treat us, we create a space where our emotions are valued and respected. Remember that asserting yourself does not make you selfish; it demonstrates self-love and self-respect. Take this opportunity to prioritize yourself by embracing the power of healthy boundaries in all aspects of your life

CHAPTER 19: THE POWER OF MINDFUL LISTENING

As we navigate through the intricate webs of our relationships, there is one skill that often gets overlooked but holds immense transformative power - the art of mindful listening. In a world filled with constant distractions and superficial conversations, truly listening to others has become a rare and precious gift. It is through this practice that we can strengthen our connections, foster empathy, and deepen our understanding of both ourselves and those around us.

Mindful listening goes beyond simply hearing words; it involves being fully present in the moment with an open heart and an open mind. When we engage in mindful listening, we create a safe space for others to share their thoughts, emotions, and vulnerabilities without fear of judgment or interruption. This act of presence allows us to connect on a deeper level with those we care about.

To cultivate the art of mindful listening requires us to shift our focus from ourselves to the speaker. It means setting aside our own agendas, opinions, and preconceived notions while immersing ourselves fully in their story or perspective. By doing so, we not only validate their experience but also gain valuable insights into their inner world.

In order to practice mindful listening effectively, we must let go of distractions that hinder our ability to be fully present. This means putting aside electronic devices, turning off notifications, and creating a physical environment conducive to deep connection. By eliminating external interruptions, we can give undivided attention to the person speaking.

Active listening is another crucial element in mindful communication. It involves not only hearing what is being said but also observing body language and non-verbal cues that accompany the spoken words. Paying attention to these subtleties allows us to understand not just what someone is saying but also how they are feeling.

When engaging in active listening, it's important to remember that our role as listeners is not to provide solutions or advice unless explicitly asked for. Often people just need someone to lend an empathetic ear, a safe space to express themselves without fear of judgment or criticism. By resisting the urge to interject with our own opinions, we create an environment conducive to authentic and meaningful communication.

Mindful listening also requires us to practice self-awareness. It demands that we become aware of our own biases, assumptions, and tendencies to interrupt or jump to conclusions. By recognizing these patterns within ourselves, we can consciously choose to let go of them and approach conversations with a beginner's mind - free from preconceived notions.

In the practice of mindful listening, silence plays a pivotal role. Embracing moments of silence allows both the speaker and the listener time for reflection and introspection. It creates a space for thoughts and emotions to settle, leading to deeper insights and more profound connections.

As we strive for mindful listening in our relationships, it is important not only to apply this skill with others but also towards ourselves. Taking time for self-reflection and introspection allows us to become better listeners not only externally but internally as well. By tuning inwards, we can gain clarity about our own emotions, thoughts, and needs - enabling us to show up more authentically in our interactions with others.

Practicing mindful listening is not always easy; it requires intentionality, effort, and patience. However, the rewards far outweigh the challenges. Through this practice, we can cultivate stronger bonds with loved ones by fostering genuine understanding and empathy.

So let us embark on this journey together - a journey towards understanding that when others speak or judge us harshly; they are often projecting their own insecurities onto us rather than truly judging who we are as individuals. By becoming masters of mindful listening, we can break free from these judgments both within ourselves and in others' perceptions of us.

Remember that each conversation is an opportunity for growth; an invitation into someone else's world where mutual understanding thrives. Let us embrace the power of mindful listening and witness the transformation it brings to our relationships, our lives, and ultimately, ourselves.

CHAPTER 20: FINDING STRENGTH IN VULNERABILITY

In this chapter, we will explore the concept of vulnerability and how it can be a source of strength and authenticity. We often associate vulnerability with weakness, but in reality, it takes immense courage to show up as our true selves and embrace our vulnerabilities.

Vulnerability is not about being defenseless or exposing ourselves to harm; it is about allowing ourselves to be seen, heard, and understood. It requires us to let go of the masks we wear and the walls we build around us. When we open ourselves up to vulnerability, we create an opportunity for deep connections and genuine relationships.

Recognizing vulnerability as a source of strength is not an easy task. Society often encourages us to hide our vulnerabilities and project an image of invincibility. However, by embracing our vulnerabilities, we tap into a wellspring of authenticity that can transform our lives.

When we have the courage to show up as our true selves, despite the fear of judgment or rejection, we establish a foundation for resilience. Resilience is not about bouncing back from adversity unscathed; it is about navigating challenges with grace and using them as catalysts for growth.

Building resilience through vulnerability requires us to cultivate self-compassion. We must learn to treat ourselves with kindness when faced with setbacks or failures. Instead of berating ourselves for our imperfections, we should acknowledge them as part of what makes us human.

As I reflect upon my own journey towards understanding vulnerability's power, I am reminded of a time when I felt compelled to hide my true self out of fear. I was attending a social event where I believed everyone would judge me based on my appearance or social status. As a result, I put on a facade - projecting an image that was far from authentic.

However, one person saw through my charade - Sarah. She approached me with genuine curiosity and asked me questions that went beyond superficial small talk. In that moment, I realized she wasn't judging me; she was judging herself. She too had fears and insecurities, and by opening up to vulnerability, she created a safe space for others to do the same.

Sarah's example inspired me to embrace vulnerability as a strength rather than a weakness. I began to share my thoughts, feelings, and experiences with those around me - not seeking validation but striving for authentic connections. Through this process, I discovered that vulnerability is not only empowering but also liberating.

When we allow ourselves to be vulnerable, we invite others to do the same. It creates a ripple effect that encourages authenticity in our relationships and fosters an environment where people can truly be themselves. We no longer have to fear judgment or rejection because we understand that when someone judges us, they are simply projecting their own insecurities onto us.

Vulnerability is not something to be feared or hidden; it is a wellspring of strength and authenticity waiting to be tapped into. By embracing our vulnerabilities and showing up as our true selves, we build resilience and create meaningful connections with others.

So let us embrace vulnerability with open hearts and open minds - knowing that when we allow ourselves to be seen for who we truly are, we inspire others to do the same. Remember, they aren't judging you; they are judging themselves. And through vulnerability, we can break free from the chains of judgment and experience true liberation.

CHAPTER 21: EMBRACING THE JOURNEY OF SELF-DISCOVERY

In our quest for self-understanding, we often find ourselves on a transformative journey of self-discovery. It is a voyage that takes us deep within, unraveling the layers of our being and shedding light on the true essence of who we are. This chapter explores this profound expedition, as we challenge the limiting beliefs that have held us back and embrace new truths about ourselves.

Embarking on this journey requires courage, for it demands that we confront our fears, insecurities, and doubts head-on. It beckons us to step outside our comfort zones and delve into the uncharted territories of our souls. The path may be arduous at times, but with each step forward, we inch closer to unlocking the hidden treasures buried within us.

To embark on this transformative odyssey, we must first recognize the limiting beliefs that have hindered our growth. These beliefs are like invisible chains that keep us confined to a narrow perception of ourselves. They whisper destructive narratives in our minds, convincing us that we are unworthy or incapable.

The journey starts by challenging these beliefs—an act of rebellion against their oppressive grip. We must question their validity and examine how they have shaped our thoughts and actions throughout our lives. By doing so, we gain clarity about their origins and begin to dismantle their power over us.

As we shed these self-imposed limitations, a newfound freedom emerges—a liberation from the shackles that once held us captive in a limited version of ourselves. With each belief shattered, space opens up for new possibilities to bloom within us.

However, embracing these new truths about ourselves is not an easy feat either. Often it requires confronting aspects of ourselves that we may have been avoiding or denying for years. It means accepting both our strengths and weaknesses with compassion and understanding.

In this process of self-acceptance lies an opportunity for transformational growth. By acknowledging our flaws and imperfections, we open the door to self-improvement and personal evolution. It is through understanding our weaknesses that we can harness our strengths more effectively, allowing us to become the best versions of ourselves.

This journey of self-discovery also invites us to explore uncharted territories within our passions, interests, and desires. As we peel back the layers of societal expectations and external influences, we unearth the authentic desires that reside deep within us.

Perhaps there is a hidden artist longing to express itself through paintbrush strokes or a dormant adventurer yearning for thrilling escapades. By embracing these passions and allowing ourselves to pursue them with abandon, we tap into a wellspring of fulfillment and joy that enriches every aspect of our lives.

Along this transformative journey, it is crucial to extend ourselves compassion and patience. Self-discovery is not a linear process; it ebbs and flows like the tides of an ocean. There will be moments of clarity and moments of confusion, times when we feel grounded in who we are and times when we question everything.

In these challenging moments, it is essential to remember that self-discovery is not about reaching a final destination but rather about embracing the lifelong process of growth. It requires curiosity, openness, and a willingness to explore all facets of ourselves—the light as well as the shadow.

As we venture deeper into this exploration, something magical happens—we begin to realize that others' judgments no longer hold power over us. We recognize that they are merely projecting their own insecurities onto us—a reflection of their own internal battles rather than an accurate measurement of our worth.

Understanding this liberates us from the fear of judgment because now we comprehend that judgment says more about them than it does about us. We can move forward confidently on our path knowing that authenticity trumps conformity every time.

The journey to self-discovery may be daunting at times; it may require confronting uncomfortable truths or embracing aspects of ourselves we have long denied. But it is within this transformative adventure that we find the essence of our being—the truest version of ourselves.

So, dear reader, I invite you to embark on this journey with an open heart and a curious mind. Embrace the challenges, let go of limiting beliefs, and pursue your passions fearlessly. For in doing so, you will uncover a profound understanding—that they aren't judging you; they're judging themselves. And in understanding this truth, you will set yourself free to live authentically and wholeheartedly.

CHAPTER 22: THE POWER OF SELF-REFLECTION

In our journey towards understanding ourselves and others, there is a powerful tool that often goes unnoticed - the practice of self-reflection. Engaging in regular self-reflection allows us to gain deeper insights into our thoughts and behaviors, providing us with an opportunity for personal growth and transformation.

Self-reflection is a process of introspection, where we take the time to examine our own thoughts, emotions, and actions. It is not about judging ourselves but rather about gaining awareness and understanding. By shining a light on our inner world, we can uncover hidden patterns, beliefs, and motivations that shape how we interact with ourselves and the world around us.

One might wonder why self-reflection is necessary when there are external sources of feedback available to us. While feedback from others can be valuable, it often comes from their own perspectives and judgments. On the other hand, self-reflection provides us with an unbiased lens through which we can explore our own experiences without external influence.

To engage in effective self-reflection, it is important to create a quiet space where you can be alone with your thoughts. Find a comfortable place free from distractions where you can truly focus on yourself. This could be a cozy corner in your home or a peaceful spot in nature.

Once you have found your space, give yourself permission to fully immerse in the process of self-reflection. Let go of any expectations or judgments you may have about what should arise during this time. The goal is simply to observe and understand yourself better.

Begin by taking deep breaths and grounding yourself in the present moment. Close your eyes if it helps you connect with your inner self. Allow your mind to wander freely as memories surface or emotions arise.

As you dive into the depths of your consciousness during this practice, pay attention to any recurring patterns or themes that emerge. Notice if certain situations trigger specific emotional responses within you. Explore the beliefs and assumptions that underlie your thoughts and actions.

Remember, self-reflection is not about criticizing or blaming yourself. It is about developing self-awareness and compassion. Treat yourself with kindness and understanding as you navigate through your inner landscape.

To enhance the effectiveness of your self-reflection practice, consider keeping a journal. Writing down your thoughts, feelings, and insights can provide clarity and help you track your progress over time. This will also serve as a valuable resource for future reflection.

While it can be challenging to confront our own shadows and

vulnerabilities, it is through this process that we can truly grow and transform. By embracing our imperfections with compassion, we open ourselves up to the possibility of change.

Self-reflection also allows us to break free from the cycle of judgment towards others. As we gain a deeper understanding of ourselves, we realize that when others judge us, they are often projecting their own insecurities onto us. Understanding this helps us cultivate empathy towards others instead of taking their judgments personally.

The practice of self-reflection holds immense power in our journey towards personal growth and transformation. By engaging in regular self-reflection, we gain deeper insights into our thoughts and behaviors without external influence or judgment. Through compassionate exploration of our inner world, we uncover hidden patterns and beliefs that shape how we interact with ourselves and others. So take a moment to pause amidst the chaos of life, create space for self-reflection, and watch as you embark on a transformative journey towards understanding yourself better.

CHAPTER 23: EMBRACING IMPERFECTIONS AND PRACTICING RADICAL ACCEPTANCE

In this chapter, we delve into the profound art of radical acceptance, exploring how it can lead us to a place of self-love and self-compassion. We will discover that by embracing our imperfections as integral parts of our wholeness, we can free ourselves from the burden of judgment and find peace within.

Life is a journey filled with ups and downs, triumphs and failures. Along this winding path, we often encounter moments where we feel inadequate or flawed. Society bombards us with images of perfection, setting impossibly high standards for beauty, success, and happiness. It's easy to fall into the trap of comparing ourselves to others or striving for an ideal that can never truly be attained.

But what if we shifted our perspective? What if we recognized that our imperfections are not flaws but rather unique aspects that make us who we are? What if we acknowledged that our struggles are not signs of weakness but opportunities for growth?

Embracing imperfections requires a radical shift in mindset—a willingness to let go of societal expectations and embrace our authentic selves. It starts with acknowledging that perfection is an illusion constructed by external forces. True beauty lies not in flawlessness but in authenticity.

To practice radical acceptance is to look within ourselves with kindness and understanding. It means acknowledging the times when we stumble or fall short without berating ourselves for it. Instead of dwelling on perceived failures, it involves recognizing them as stepping stones toward personal growth.

Imagine a world where instead of judging ourselves harshly for every mistake made or flaw discovered, we celebrated these moments as opportunities for self-improvement—a world where grace replaces criticism and compassion replaces condemnation.

Radical acceptance also extends beyond embracing our own imperfections; it necessitates extending understanding towards others as well. When someone judges us harshly or criticizes us unfairly, it is often a reflection of their own insecurities and self-judgment. By recognizing this, we can choose not to internalize their judgment or allow it to define our worth.

In the face of judgment, we have a choice—to let it wound us or to respond with empathy and understanding. When we understand that the judgments cast upon us are merely projections of someone else's inner struggles, their impact diminishes. We can cultivate compassion for those who judge us, knowing that they are fighting their own battles.

Practicing radical acceptance is not easy; it requires patience and self-compassion. But the rewards are immeasurable. When we accept ourselves and others with all our imperfections, we create space for growth, healing, and genuine connection.

So how do we embark on this journey of radical acceptance? It begins by cultivating self-awareness—observing our thoughts, emotions, and reactions without judgment. Through mindfulness practices such as meditation or journaling, we can develop a deeper understanding of ourselves and uncover hidden beliefs or patterns that contribute to self-judgment.

With this newfound awareness comes the power to challenge these beliefs—to replace self-criticism with self-compassion. We can start reframing negative thoughts into positive affirmations —reminding ourselves that imperfection is not a flaw but an opportunity for growth.

Additionally, seeking support from trusted friends or professionals can be invaluable on this journey. Sharing our struggles with others who understand without judgment can provide comfort and guidance as we navigate the path towards radical acceptance.

As we embrace our imperfections as integral parts of our wholeness and practice radical acceptance towards ourselves and others alike, a profound transformation occurs within us—a shift from self-judgment to self-love; from criticism to compassion.

Understanding that they aren't judging you but rather judging themselves is a powerful realization on the path toward radical acceptance. By embracing our imperfections as integral parts of our wholeness and practicing self-love and self-compassion, we can free ourselves from the burden of judgment and find true peace within. Let us embark on this transformative journey together, supporting one another as we navigate the beautiful art of radical acceptance.

CHAPTER 24: NURTURING SELF-CONNECTION

In this chapter, we will explore the importance of building a strong connection with ourselves through self-care and self-compassion. It is through nurturing self-connection that we can find inner harmony and balance in our lives.

Self-connection is about developing a deep understanding and acceptance of who we are as individuals. It involves acknowledging our strengths, weaknesses, desires, and fears without judgment or criticism. When we nurture our self-connection, we create a safe space within ourselves where we can explore our thoughts and emotions freely.

One way to nurture self-connection is through practicing self-care. Self-care involves actively taking care of our physical, emotional, and mental well-being. It means making time for activities that bring us joy, relaxation, and rejuvenation. Whether it's taking a long bath, going for a walk in nature, or simply curling up with a good book; engaging in activities that nourish our soul helps strengthen our connection with ourselves.

Another essential aspect of nurturing self-connection is practicing self-compassion. Self-compassion is the act of treating ourselves with kindness and understanding when faced with difficulties or setbacks. Instead of berating ourselves for perceived failures or mistakes, we offer ourselves the same compassion we would extend to a dear friend.

To cultivate self-compassion, it's crucial to recognize that everyone makes mistakes and experiences challenges in life—it's part of being human. By embracing this truth and reframing how we perceive failure, we can foster an environment of kindness towards ourselves.

Reflecting upon the transcript provided as inspiration for this chapter:

We learn from the transcript that building a strong connection with oneself requires nurturing practices such as mindfulness meditation or journaling exercises that encourage introspection. These practices allow us to delve deeper into our thoughts and emotions while promoting an increased sense of awareness.

Furthermore, the transcript emphasizes the importance of acknowledging that when others judge or criticize us, it is often a reflection of their own insecurities and self-judgment. Understanding this can help alleviate the burden we may feel when faced with judgment from others.

In order to nurture self-connection, it is essential to create boundaries that protect our emotional well-being. This means being mindful of the relationships we engage in and surrounding ourselves with individuals who support and uplift us rather than bring us down.

Lastly, embracing vulnerability plays a significant role in nurturing self-connection. This involves allowing ourselves to be authentic and open with our thoughts, feelings, and experiences. By embracing vulnerability, we invite genuine connections into our lives and foster a deeper understanding of ourselves.

Nurturing self-connection is an ongoing journey that requires conscious effort and practice. It involves engaging in self-care activities that bring us joy and actively practicing self-compassion when faced with challenges or setbacks. By cultivating these habits, we strengthen our connection with ourselves and create an inner harmony that radiates into all aspects of our lives.

Now armed with the knowledge presented in this chapter, readers can embark on their own journey of nurturing self-connection. By prioritizing self-care, practicing self-compassion, setting healthy boundaries, embracing vulnerability, and reframing their perception of judgment from others; they will unlock the power within themselves to find true inner peace and understanding.

CHAPTER 25: THE POWER OF RESILIENCE

In the face of adversity, it is often our ability to bounce back that determines our success. Life throws curveballs at us, testing our strength and resolve. It is during these challenging times that the power of resilience becomes evident.

Resilience is not an innate quality that some are born with, and others lack. It is a skill that can be developed through the practice of self-compassion and self-care. When we treat ourselves with kindness and understanding, we build a solid foundation for resilience.

One way to cultivate resilience is by embracing challenges as opportunities for growth. Instead of viewing setbacks as failures, we can reframe them as valuable learning experiences. This shift in perspective allows us to approach difficulties with a sense of curiosity and openness, rather than fear or frustration.

Consider the story of Emily, a young woman who faced numerous obstacles on her path to success. Instead of succumbing to despair when she encountered setbacks, Emily embraced each challenge as an opportunity for personal growth. She recognized that failure was not a reflection of her worth but rather an indication that she was pushing herself outside her comfort zone.

Through self-compassion and self-care practices such as meditation, journaling, and seeking support from loved ones, Emily built up her resilience over time. She learned to acknowledge her emotions without judgment and to treat herself with kindness during difficult moments.

As Emily's resilience grew stronger, she found herself better equipped to handle even the toughest situations life threw at her. Rather than crumbling under pressure, she thrived in adversity by tapping into her inner strength and resourcefulness.

Resilience also involves developing effective coping mechanisms in times of stress or trauma. One way to achieve this is by cultivating mindfulness – the practice of being fully present in the moment without judgment or attachment.

Mindfulness enables us to observe our thoughts and emotions without getting caught up in them. By cultivating awareness of our inner experiences, we can better understand how they influence our reactions to external events. This self-awareness allows us to choose more adaptive responses when faced with adversity, enhancing our resilience.

Take a moment to reflect on your own experiences. How have you responded to challenges in the past? Have you approached them with self-compassion and an open mind? Or have you allowed fear and self-doubt to hold you back?

If you find yourself struggling to bounce back from setbacks, know that resilience is not a fixed trait but rather a skill that can be cultivated. Begin by practicing self-compassion – treating yourself with the same kindness and understanding you would extend to a dear friend facing difficulties.

Additionally, prioritize self-care activities that nourish your mind, body, and soul. Engage in activities that bring you joy and relaxation, whether it's taking a long walk in nature, reading a good book, or spending quality time with loved ones.

Remember, building resilience takes time and effort. It is not about avoiding challenges but rather developing the skills necessary to face them head-on. Embrace setbacks as opportunities for growth and approach them with curiosity and openness.

The power of resilience lies within each of us. By cultivating self-compassion, embracing challenges as opportunities for growth, and developing effective coping mechanisms like mindfulness, we can strengthen our ability to bounce back from adversity. So remember: they aren't judging you; they are judging themselves. Focus on your own journey of growth and let resilience guide you towards success.

CHAPTER 26: THE JOURNEY TO SELF-LOVE

As we continue on our path of self-discovery and personal growth, one essential aspect that we must embrace is the concept of self-love. Far too often, we find ourselves caught in a cycle of self-judgment and criticism, constantly comparing ourselves to others and feeling inadequate. However, it is crucial to realize that the judgments we perceive from others are often projections of their own insecurities and fears.

Embracing self-love requires us to recognize our true worth and potential. It is an act of kindness and compassion towards ourselves, acknowledging that we are deserving of love, respect, and acceptance. This journey towards self-love may not be an easy one, but it is undoubtedly a transformative process that can lead us to a place of peace, fulfillment, and happiness.

To begin this journey, we must first understand that the judgments we perceive from others are not a reflection of our own value or worthiness. Instead, they stem from their own internal struggles. Just as we have our insecurities and doubts, so do they. When someone judges us harshly or criticizes our choices or appearance, it is often because they are projecting their own fears onto us.

By recognizing this truth, we can free ourselves from the burden of external judgment. We can choose not to internalize these criticisms but instead view them as opportunities for growth and understanding – both for ourselves and for those who project their insecurities onto us.

Self-love also involves accepting ourselves fully – flaws and all. It requires embracing every aspect of who we are – the good parts along with the perceived shortcomings. Rather than striving for perfection or trying to meet society's unrealistic standards, self-love encourages us to appreciate our uniqueness.

Through introspection and reflection, we can identify our strengths and weaknesses objectively without judgment or comparison with others. By acknowledging our vulnerabilities without shame or guilt, we open ourselves up to growth and self-improvement. Self-love teaches us that imperfections are what make us human, and they should be celebrated rather than hidden away.

In this journey towards self-love, it is essential to surround ourselves with supportive and loving individuals. Seeking out those who uplift us, encourage our growth, and believe in our potential can significantly impact our ability to cultivate self-love. These individuals serve as mirrors, reflecting back the love and acceptance that we deserve.

Additionally, practicing self-care plays a vital role in this journey. Taking the time to prioritize our physical, emotional, and mental well-being allows us to nurture ourselves fully. Engaging in activities that bring joy or pursuing hobbies that ignite passion helps us reconnect with ourselves on a deeper level.

Self-love also involves setting healthy boundaries – both with ourselves and others. It means recognizing when we need alone time or space for introspection without feeling guilty about it. It also means respecting our own needs and desires while asserting them confidently but respectfully with others.

Throughout this journey of self-love, there will undoubtedly be obstacles and setbacks along the way. We may find ourselves slipping into old patterns of negative self-talk or comparing ourselves to others once again. However, these moments should not be seen as failures but rather as opportunities for growth.

The road to self-love is not linear; it is a continuous process of learning, unlearning, and relearning how to care for ourselves unconditionally. Each step we take towards embracing our worthiness brings us closer to living a life filled with love – both for ourselves and for others.

Understanding that the judgments we perceive from others are not about us but reflections of their own insecurities allows us to embark on the transformative journey of self-love. By accepting ourselves fully – flaws included – surrounding ourselves with supportive individuals who believe in our potential, practicing self-care diligently while setting healthy boundaries, and navigating setbacks with grace and resilience, we can cultivate a deep sense of self-love that radiates in every aspect of our lives.

DESIRED IMPACT FOR READERS:

Upon reading "They Are Judging You, They Are Judging Themselves," readers will experience a profound shift in perspective and a deepening sense of self-awareness. By internalizing the book's teachings on self-compassion, forgiveness, and authenticity, readers will embark on a transformative journey toward inner peace and personal growth.

Through reflection and practice, readers will learn to recognize the ways in which their perceptions of others are often mirrors of their own inner struggles. Armed with this understanding, they will break free from the cycle of self-criticism and cultivate a greater sense of compassion and empathy, both for themselves and others.

As readers integrate the book's principles into their daily lives, they will find themselves navigating relationships with newfound grace and understanding. They will embrace vulnerability as a source of strength, courageously showing up as their authentic selves in every interaction.

Ultimately, the desired impact of "They Are Judging You, They Are Judging Themselves" is to empower readers to live more fulfilling and authentic lives. By embracing self-compassion, practicing forgiveness, and fostering genuine connections, readers will cultivate a deep sense of inner peace and fulfillment that radiates outward, positively impacting every aspect of their lives.

ABOUT THE AUTHOR

Adrianne Muntz is a compassionate and dedicated professional with a diverse background in helping individuals and families navigate life's challenges. Holding a Master's degree in Clinical Social Work, Adrianne has committed her career to supporting others in overcoming obstacles and finding greater happiness and well-being. As a certified autism informed specialist, she brings a unique understanding and sensitivity to her work, ensuring that individuals with autism receive tailored support and care.

In addition to her role as a Clinical Social Worker, Adrianne is skilled in mediation services, facilitating effective communication and peaceful resolutions to conflicts within families. Her commitment to ensuring that everyone's voices are heard and respected is at the forefront of her practice.

Adrianne's expertise extends beyond clinical work –she is also certified in Project Management. This additional skill set allows her to plan and execute initiatives that merge health justice and social justice, empowering families to make decisions that positively impact their long-term well-being.

Passionate about making a tangible difference in her community, Adrianne owns a wellness business focused on promoting emotional well-being and holistic health. Through this venture, she offers a range of products and services designed to help individuals and families thrive in all aspects of their lives.

Driven by a vision of a more supportive and equitable society,

Adrianne is committed to empowering individuals with coping strategies, self-awareness techniques, and relaxation methods. She believes in fostering a culture of wellness within families and communities, making therapy accessible and empowering for everyone.

In today's world, where emotional health is more crucial than ever, Adrianne Muntz is at the forefront of creating a brighter future where individuals and families can find the support they need to live happier, healthier lives.